ISBN 978-1-4466-2844-7

This book is dedicated to my

husband, best friend and soul mate.

I love the way that we have become better at being one

over the years.

*Gen 2:24 Therefore a man shall leave his father and his
mother and hold fast to his wife, and they shall become one flesh.*

Acknowledgements

Many thanks to my Mom, who spent many hours
making my content more readable.

Thanks to my two proof readers,

Julia Baker and Angie Hope.

Thanks to all of my friends who encouraged

me to keep going with this project.

Contents

Foreward

by Evan Rogers

Many of us will stand at the altar of marriage and make the familiar vows: 'til death us do part', 'in sickness and in health' or 'for better or for worse'.

Offspring from marriage is assumed and expected as a natural result of this union. What if 'with children or without children' was included?

As a young married couple, little did we know that these promises would become very real and the expected would become the unexpected, a consistent challenge and life-long journey.

Foreward

My courageous, brave and beautiful wife has decided to tell our story in a frank, honest and detailed account. She has decided to place the private into the public. 'No Kid-ing' serves to bring some purpose to the pain.

This book has proved to be cathartic for her but will also be a great help in getting this ever increasing challenge of living a childless life spoken about. Tracy doesn't try to give any answers but simply shares her thoughts and tells her story. This book gives the reader a moment to identify, experience and appreciate the challenges of a woman in pursuit of a life-long desire. Tracy has always 'said it as it is' and regardless of your views on the issues around infertility she sets out to simply let you walk our road.

Chapter One

The History of Evan and Tracy

This is the story of Evan's and my quest to have children, but first some history.

When I think back to my childhood, I can remember being quite a tomboy. I had a cowboy outfit and a superman one, but I also had dolls. The first doll that I can remember, I named Tammy. Later a new model came out that could drink water, cry tears and wet her nappy – time for an addition to the family, her name was Nicky. Next came a doll that looked incredibly similar to a newborn baby, I think it was called a 'Baby

Angel'. I named my third 'daughter' Sally-Ann. We had a funny experience … we'd gone for a walk with the family and I had got tired of carrying Sally-Ann, so my father was carrying her by her leg and we got a hilarious reaction from some passersby who thought it was a real baby! When they discovered that it was a doll, we got some good laughs of relief!

When I was in primary school, I wanted to be a teacher. Back then we didn't have any of these fancy simulator games, so my poor younger brother, John and his friends had to be the pupils in my 'teacher-teacher' game. One of John's friends insisted on writing in the margins and it used to make me crazy. Looking back, he probably just did it to wind me up! I can't believe they had the patience to play the game with me. I must have had some excellent classroom control.

When I got to Grade Eight, I had to do a school project

on my family history and the last bit was to write about what you wanted in your future. I said that I wanted to live on a big piece of land with lots of dogs and have four children - a boy, twin girls and then another boy. That was when I was twelve years old and that is what I have continued to desire throughout my life.

When I grew out of dolls, it was time for boyfriends. My brother, John is a year younger than me and was always very protective over my choice of boys. At first, I was only allowed to have his friends as boyfriends. So my first pre-teen boyfriend was his best friend! When I got older and wanted to choose my own boyfriends, we had some problems. By this stage I had followed John into the wonderful sport of surfing. Unfortunately surfing does attract some rather unsavoury characters, so John had his work cut out for him!

We used to spend every weekend and holiday in

Muizenberg and if we weren't in the water catching waves, we were hanging out in Shorebreak, the local pool joint. There were various 'potential' relationships dotted along the way during my surfing days but none of them came together as even though at times it was hard, deep down inside I knew that only a Christian relationship would work out long-term for me.

By the age of sixteen most of my school friends were in relationships and I was feeling quite desperate for a boyfriend. Sweet sixteen and never been kissed!

My mother had trained John and me to seek answers from God in important situations. I remember asking God for a word from the Bible about when I would get a boyfriend and when I opened it up, the first word that I saw on the page was 'soon'! How funny when I think back, but it did comfort me!

No Kid-ing

Shortly after that, a good looking guy started visiting our church. He was a surfer, Christian and amazingly had John's approval! He was four years older than me, and had nearly finished college so I didn't really hold out much hope. I remember seeing him for the first time when he and his group of friends visited Summer Camp, it was love at first sight! He started coming to our church regularly and we had similar friends, so ended up going to a few social events together. He very cleverly befriended my brother and asked if he could take us surfing.

Having met Evan for the first time at a New Year's Eve party, a few weeks later, on the 23rd January 1988 we were dating. He was quite serious right from the start. I remember him telling me that he only believed in dating girls he could see a future with. As for me, I was more than delighted to be in a serious relationship with a hot Christian surfer! Being Christians, we believed that sex was for married couples and had a frustrating four year wait before we could get married and be sexually intimate. I think that was the only problem with meeting my future marriage partner so young!

Evan is a song-writer, so he proposed to me in a song. He took me to our favourite dinner/dance restaurant and after supper, when 'Lady in Red' was playing, he asked me to dance. I was a little bit reluctant as there was no-one else on the dance floor but he managed to persuade me. After the first song, I was completely taken by surprise to hear Evan's voice singing the next song, 'Will You Marry Me' …

'Will you marry me, will you let me be

Your lover and your friend?

With this ring I pledge my will to wed

And love you till the end.'

No Kid-ing

Four months later, on the 14th December 1991, we got married. Evan's best man and housemate had joked with us not to forget our contraceptives. We were driving to the first stop-off on our honeymoon and saw that my toiletry bag was not in the car. Pills left behind – oh dear! We had to turn around and go and fetch them. Funny when we think back now to how unnecessary they were!

Chapter Two

Nesting

Our first family home was a two-bedroomed flat which we had bought a year prior to getting married. Initially we rented it out and later Evan and our friend, Mike lived in it.

I was so excited to get home from honeymoon so that we could open all of our wedding presents and start 'nesting'. This was the fulfillment of a life-long dream for me. I had to do my home-making on a limited budget as I was a second year university student, studying BSc, majoring in Mathematics and in

Nesting

Environmental and Geographical Science and Evan was a Grade Six Primary School teacher. Down the line my passion for Maths ultimately led me into becoming a High School Maths teacher, which I thought would be a career that would be complementary to my dream of having a big family. My plan had always been to be a stay-at-home mom and possibly return to teaching once my children were of school-going age.

After four years of Primary School teaching, Evan, whose passion had always been music, was offered a position as the Music Director in our church, Jubilee. This gave him the opportunity to leave teaching and pursue his dream. It freed up time for him to write songs and record and over the years he has produced many albums.

Once I had qualified as a teacher, we were in a position where we could secure a bigger mortgage and consider selling our flat and buying a house. As soon as this process was set in motion, we could no longer wait to get our first dog and thought that she would survive a few weeks in a flat! We went to the local Animal Rescue and both immediately fell for a Ridgeback-cross puppy. We couldn't wait to complete the necessary paperwork and take our new puppy, Chandler, home!

Chapter Three

The quest begins

We started trying for kids in the November of ′96 after five years of marriage. That was always the plan. I had just turned twenty-five and we had finished paying off my student loan. We had bought a two bed-roomed cottage and thought it was a good time to start expanding the family. After three months of no success, being the rather impatient person that I am, I thought I should go for a check-up with a gynaecologist.

I went to Dr Sandler who examined me and couldn't find anything seriously wrong with me. He did, however, send me for a blood test and based on these results he thought that there was a slight possibility that I was not ovulating properly. He prescribed a fertility drug called Clomid which helps to stimulate the ovaries to produce eggs, lots of them! When we saw the price of the Clomid we realised that this was going to be an expensive journey.

That month I had to go for a scan to check if the Clomid had done its trick. In the scan I could see that there were a number of follicles (where the egg forms) and Dr Sandler was happy with the result. At this stage I was very excited as multiple pregnancies had been mentioned and I had always wanted twins.

Naturally Evan and I had high hopes for that month but I got my dreaded period. We were quite devastated, but still believed that there would be a solution for us. Growing up as the daughter of a doctor, I had great faith in the ability of the medical profession to come up with answers in challenging situations.

Dr Sandler suggested that Evan go for a sperm test. We were excited in that it was a new route to investigate and hopefully one that would come up with a constructive way forward. I was teaching at Westerford High School at the time and had to call for the results during a break time. I was distressed by what I heard and ran straight to the bathroom and cried. I was told that Evan had a very low sperm count and low percentage of good sperm.

We had only shared our situation with close family at this stage and I felt the need to find someone who would be able to relate to what we were going through. We knew a couple in our church who had tried unsuccessfully to have children and thought it would be good to get together with them and compare notes.

The quest begins

They were very encouraging as they thought that they had left their medical intervention too late and that we had a great advantage because we had found the problem at such an early stage.

It is amazing how different our lives are now with unlimited access to information through the internet. It would have been so helpful for me at that particular moment to have been able to find out more about our dilemma and find similar stories via medical websites, blogs and forums.

Based on the results of the sperm test, Dr Sandler had referred Evan to an urologist, Dr Nicolle to see if anything could be done surgically to improve the quality and count of the sperm. Evan went for the appointment and came back most discouraged. The doctor had told him to consider adoption or using donor sperm. He didn't seem to hold out much hope for our quest.

No Kid-ing

This was the first time that we had come face to face with the possibility that we might never have our own biological children. A truly devastating thought.

Chapter Four

The next step

After Dr Nicolle's initially negative prognosis, he suggested that Evan have a testicular biopsy to check that there was no blockage hindering sperm production or any other concerning issues. The surgical procedure was a painful one. The results were good, but the test didn't reveal any new obstacle that could be overcome.

He suggested that Evan take Clomid for three months, a fairly innovative treatment at the time, as previously it had only been used to resolve female infertility issues.

The next step

We then had to wait a further three months, followed by another sperm test to see if there was any improvement.

During this time I had decided to take a six month break from running as so many people had told me or implied that running was the reason we weren't conceiving. Even though I knew this to be untrue, having asked the doctors, I thought I would try it anyway, if just to prove to a few people that it was not the issue. It only becomes one, as a sportsperson, if your body fat drops so low that you stop having your period because you are no longer ovulating. This was never a problem for me.

This takes us to the beginning of 1998, just over a year since our journey began. When I called for the results of the sperm test, Dr Nicolle said that the Clomid had not had a significant effect and he recommended that we see a fertility specialist. At this point, my hope of having our own biological children was restored as previously we had been led to believe that this last test would be the end of the road as far as that was concerned.

Dr Nicolle recommended some specialists, among whom, was a Dr Alperstein. I'd met him before, as I had taught his daughter at Westerford and he'd attended a parent-teacher meeting. I remembered him as being someone who commanded my respect and was keen to consult with him. My father, who knew him, was happy to contact him and try to get an appointment on our behalf. He explained to Dr Alperstein that Evan was working for the church and so he kindly agreed to treat us for free. He also said that he would like to see us as soon as possible, which was encouraging as the waiting list for appointments with fertility specialists was normally quite long.

The next step

Evan and I went together for our appointment and he told us that he would like to try three Artificial Inseminations (A.I). He told us that they would 'wash' Evan's sperm and inject the best ones into me at ovulation. We had our first A.I. in April 1998. I had to start taking Clomid again. On the tenth day of my cycle, I had to go for a scan to assess the follicle development and on ovulation day I had an injection which stimulated the follicles to release the eggs. Evan had to produce a sperm sample which went to the Newlands Fertility Clinic to be washed.

After having had to produce a sample before in the bathroom of Doctor's rooms, he was told that he could produce the sample in the comfort of his home as long as he rushed it to the clinic immediately after. At that stage he was driving a scooter and said he would drive as fast and carefully as he could in order to get the sample there safely. He had nightmares of crashing and the sample being ruined!

Later in the day, Evan and I met back at Dr Alperstein's rooms where he inserted the sperm into my uterus with a catheter. It was such a weird feeling knowing that this could be the exact point at which life began to grow inside me. We were very excited!

The ten day wait before I could go for a blood test to confirm whether I was pregnant or not seemed to last forever. I kept wondering whether my usual menstrual cycle clues were perhaps signs of pregnancy, unfair that they are so similar!

The blood test revealed that I was not pregnant. We weren't too surprised because Dr Alperstein had told us that they had detected some kind of infection in Evan's sperm sample. Evan was put onto antibiotics to clear up the infection before the next attempt.

The next step

Before our next A.I in May, we were at a church camp and someone prayed for us and received a word of knowledge that there was something wrong with Evan's sperm. He prayed for healing and we were very hopeful for the second A.I. Having had the prayer backing and a non-infected sperm sample our hopes were really up! Needless to say when we found out that it also hadn't worked, we were quite broken.

In June we had our third A.I. Dr Alperstein told us that if this one didn't work, we should still try a fourth as the first one shouldn't really count because of the infection. We skipped July as we were away and had our last unsuccessful A.I in August.

I might add that by now, many of our close married friends had already had their first child. Ouch!

Chapter Five

Turning up the heat

Being as broody as I was, I managed to convince Evan
that it was time for another puppy and time to fulfill my
childhood dream of getting a Great Dane. We drove to
a farm in the countryside to fetch her. She was mostly
black and reminded us of the panther in the Jungle
Book, so we named her Bagheera, which soon got
shortened to Baggy. We took her home to meet
Chandler who seemed happy to have a playmate. In the
midst of our seemingly never-ending medical miseries,
she brought much joy and laughter into our lives.

Turning up the heat

After our fourth unsuccessful A.I, Dr Alperstein recommended that we see Prof Kruger at the Tygerberg Fertility Clinic. He was a very busy man and we only managed to get an appointment two and a half months later in November! We had a two hour session with him where he ran a number of tests on me. He did a pap smear and various blood tests.

Evan had to have a sperm test. Later he had to go back for a more sophisticated test where they simulate ovulation and see how the sperm reacts. From the results of this test, Prof Kruger deduced that we would have to have a procedure called ICSI (Intra-cytoplasmic Sperm Injection). This is a process in which they remove eggs from me and take good sperm from Evan's sample and inject the sperm into the egg to force fertilization. I could never quite get my head around how tiny the equipment used for this would have to be. Apparently the needle they use is finer than a hair!

Before we could do our first ICSI, I had to be examined again and we could only get an appointment yet another two months later, in January 1999. All of this waiting was a real test for impatient me!

Evan and I were away on our church's annual Summer Camp, but we drove the long journey from the campsite to Tygerberg Fertility Clinic at 7:15 am. I had to have an HSG, which is a radiologic procedure to investigate the shape of the uterine cavity and the fallopian tubes, and a hysteroscopy, which is the inspection of the uterine cavity by endoscopy with access through the cervix. Fortunately they didn't have to do a laparoscopy because that involves an incision. I had to go under conscious sedation. They pump air into you so that they can examine your reproductive organs.

Turning up the heat

It was quite a painful experience and I felt winded for days. It felt like I was being stabbed in the shoulder repeatedly.

Fortunately the results showed that all was healthy and Prof Kruger declared us ready to roll! I had to start sniffing Syranel nasal spray and having Perganol injections. It wasn't too pleasant to discover that Perganol is made from the urine of post menopausal women! I don't know too much about how all these drugs work, but the Pergonal was to stimulate multiple egg production. Both of these drugs will be familiar to fellow infertility sufferers. Fortunately we got the very expensive Perganol free of charge because a happy mother whose procedure had been successful had donated it to the hospital.

My good friend, Ali, who was a nurse, gave me my first injection. It was to be administered intramuscularly so I thought any muscle would be fine. We started with my upper arm. I could hardly move it the next day. The following day my father popped in and injected me in my right quad, which left me limping until bedtime. I called the hospital to find out if Perganol injections were particularly painful and was told that you are supposed to have them in your biggest muscle, that being your bottom! So the next few injections were done by various nursing sisters at the hospital where my father worked.

Driving back and forth for injections became a bit of a mission and my father lived close by, so I overcame my embarrassment and convinced him to resume injection duty.

We drove to Tygerberg Fertility Clinic, a long way from home, for three different scans during the first cycle. On one occasion I had to wait for ages to see Prof Kruger and missed a bit of school in the morning. It was quite a tricky time trying to avoid staff and school pupils' questions about my absence. I wasn't ready to tell my story at this stage.

Two days before the egg retrieval (a process called aspiration when they remove the eggs by ultrasound guided needle) my father gave me my last two Pergonal injections, one after the other. I had to go back at 11pm for him to give me a Profasi injection to induce ovulation, at which stage the follicles release the eggs. Three in one day, I was beginning to feel a bit like a pin cushion!

My first aspiration was done under sedation and it was painless. They managed to extract fourteen eggs. Evan gave a sperm sample and then the rest of the process took place in the Reproductive Unit. Only four of the eggs fertilized, but one didn't survive. They have a way of rating the embryos and we only had one good embryo and the other two were average. They put the three embryos back into my uterus three days later. It felt just like A.I – no pain. Then began the wait! Each day I had to insert cyclogests, which are shaped like tampons, but they make a horrible, sticky mess!

Once again we had to endure the wait to find out if it had worked. I was well trained in not getting my hopes up by this stage, but obviously there was a measure of eager anticipation.

As the time for my blood test to confirm pregnancy drew nearer, I found myself constantly visiting the bathroom to check if my period had arrived yet. Each time there was no negative evidence, my hopes rose a little more. On the day that I was due to have the test, I thought I'd have a quick check before making my way to the hospital and was dismayed to find the trip was no longer necessary. I called the hospital to find out if they had any idea as to why it hadn't worked and what we should do next. The nurse said quite matter-of-factly that we should try another ICSI next month. I felt like asking her if she was going to pay for it! Not being pregnant was hard enough without the additional trauma of having just wasted so much time, energy, money and enduring painful injections and invasive procedures. The whole treatment cost in excess of a month's salary, so it wasn't only the loss of a potential pregnancy, but also a financial loss.

Evan and I decided that if we were to try another procedure, God would need to provide the necessary finances.

Chapter Six

Let's try something different

At that time my mother was working for a Clinical Nutritionist who had seen a measure of success with couples struggling to have children. We made an appointment to see her. She suggested ways in which we could change our diets to enhance our chances of conceiving and improve the quality of Evan's sperm. She gave us lots of tips. She recommended that we avoided eating meat because much of it contains oestrogen which is bad for male fertility. Caffeine was also to be avoided, much to Evan, the coffee lover's dismay!

Let's try something different

She encouraged eating lots of fruit and vegetables and gave us other useful dietary guidelines. She prescribed certain helpful vitamins like zinc and other natural supplements like Lysine and Argenine for Evan. She kindly saw us free of charge, but the vitamins and supplements we had to buy were rather pricey. The Argenine, in particular, was extremely expensive in capsule form, so she said we could get it as a powder for a much better price. The only problem was that it tasted disgusting! Evan used to gulp it down with a bit of juice.

Around this time we went on our second canoeing trip down the Orange River. A colleague in the maths department at Westerford, Colleen, had organised our first trip, taking a group of pupils from the school on the river with her boyfriend, Johan's company. Over the years, Colleen and Johan have become two of our closest friends.

No Kid-ing

I recruited a group of friends and people from our
church for the second river trip. Ali and her husband,
Alister were part of the group. We had been spending a
lot of time with them as they were one of our few
remaining married friends without children. They knew
our story and had been a great support to us. When we
got to the river they both seemed unusually cautious
about the possible dangers of the trip. I kept reassuring
them that we had done it before and that there was
nothing to worry about.

Later on in the evening they told us in the most
sensitive way imaginable that Ali was pregnant. They
had been dreading telling us, knowing how raw we were
from our recent disappointment, but they didn't want
to have to appear overcautious every time we hit a rapid
for the next three days for no logical reason.

I really appreciated the way in which they told us. They
did it with such genuine compassion and care for our

feelings. It was hard for us to hear their news, not only because I wasn't pregnant yet, but also because we so wanted to have at least some married friends with children the same age as ours.

While we were away on the river we enlisted my brother, David's services as house and dog sitter. The first morning he made his breakfast and unsuspectingly added the wrong 'sugar' to his bowl. Evan's dreaded Argenine! Needless to say his cereal was ruined. He couldn't believe that Evan had to take something that tasted so disgusting. Finally, someone who could get a taste of our trials, literally!

Chapter Seven

Miraculous provision

Good friends of ours felt that God was prompting them to contribute to another ICSI and they transferred more than the needed funds into our bank account. I decided that the long journey to Tygerberg Fertility Clinic was too stressful and time-consuming so we thought we would try Newlands Fertility Clinic, which was nearer and had a very good reputation.

Tony Miles, a running friend of ours and a surgeon at the next door Newlands Surgical Clinic wanted us to see Dr Heylen, a fertility specialist. He even offered to pay the initial consultation fee for us. We felt like we were on the right track because the double financial provision at this early stage in the process seemed quite miraculous.

We went to see Dr Heylen on 1st June 1999. He was quite surprised to hear how few eggs had fertilized in my previous ICSI and said that statistically 65% usually take. He encouraged us to definitely try ICSI again and said that I had a 20% chance of having twins if I fell pregnant. Twins had always been a dream of mine and now with all the hassle of falling pregnant, I was extra keen for them or even triplets!

I then had to wait until my period started so that I could begin injections again. At the beginning of my cycle, Dr Heylen was away so I went to see his partner, Dr Wiswedel. He gave me my programme and all the necessary drugs. He asked me if I would be willing to be an egg donor, which I hadn't even considered. I thought at that stage I would rather keep all my eggs for myself! Dr Wiswedel was very positive when he saw that I was twenty-seven. He said that being young really improved my chances.

My father showed an initially reluctant Evan how to do the injections as we were going to be away in Port Elizabeth, visiting his mother for a large part of my cycle. Evan wanted my father to do the first injection and he would watch, but as Evan had to do the next day's one, I suggested that he do it and my father just supervise. I didn't want my first injection from Evan to be unsupervised! I mixed the Perganol in the syringe and Evan did a good job. Great teamwork!

This was an excellent development as now we didn't have to run around looking for nurses and clinics while away. Evan's first unsupervised injection was administered on the way to Port Elizabeth. We stopped at a roadside picnic spot in the middle of nowhere and had to try to be as discreet as possible, with cars racing by! It would have looked a rather strange sight if anyone had spotted us while driving past.

The next injection I had was at his mother's house in Port Elizabeth. We were a bit worried because it bled a little and we had been told that this could mean that we had hit a vein but all seemed fine in the end. Evan was so good with the injections as other than the one incident, he hardly made a mark! We had to cut our planned holiday short by a day as we needed to be back in time for a scan and blood test.

The waiting room of the fertility specialists became an increasingly difficult place to be as they all seemed to have hundreds of photographs of successful clients with their new babies. I would find myself sitting there and wondering why it hadn't happened for me. Maybe this time it would be my turn.

The results of the scan and blood test to check my oestrogen levels were good. Dr Wiswedel said I had a whole soccer team in my womb, so things were sounding positive! The follow-up scan showed that the follicles were growing well. Dr Wiswedel was very optimistic.

This time I also had to take progesterone pills called Utrogest. I went into Newlands Surgical Clinic at 11 am for the aspiration. They gave me three sleeping pills and an injection. I felt like I was semi-conscious and didn't feel any pain when they removed the eggs. I woke up later to find '15 beautiful eggs' written on my hand. Evan brought me home and although I still felt exhausted, I felt satisfied and slept for the rest of the day.

Miraculous provision

The following morning the lab technician from Newlands Fertility Clinic called to say that ten of the eggs had taken. We were over the moon! Dr Wiswedel was very encouraging about the embryos. He said that on their rating system, mine had scored the highest score. Good little competitive genes of mine! We told him that we were happy with a multiple pregnancy and chose to put back four embryos and freeze the other six to use in another cycle.

He inserted the embryos into my uterus and then I had to lie flat on my back in the hospital for four hours. You can imagine the thinking, hoping and praying that happened during this time! Visitors weren't allowed but fortunately for part of the time, a nurse that we knew from running was on duty, so she let my mother come and keep me company. She came for about an hour and brought a nice vegetable stir fry for Evan to make me for supper.

No Kid-ing

Once home, Evan was great and did all he could to really help me relax. Three days later I felt weird all day and didn't know whether to take it as a positive or negative sign. I lay flat most of the day and was feeling fine by the next day. I had to have another Profasi injection that night and was still on the progesterone pills. Even with all the extra hormones, I don't think I had too many mood swings. You'd have to ask Evan for a true assessment though!

A week later, ten days after the embryo implantation, I had to go for the blood test to check if I was pregnant. I went in for the test in the morning and decided to wait until I was home with Evan to call for the results. I called but Dr Wiswedel was busy so we had to wait for him to return our call. More waiting! He eventually did and much to our dismay told us that the test was negative. I was beyond tears, none of it made sense to

51

me. It had all seemed to run so smoothly both
financially and medically.

My hopes had been so high this time around. My
mother was worried that I had bottled it all up inside
but I just felt like I had already done so much crying
over the whole issue.

During procedures, the doctors recommended that I
stop heavy training but could continue easy running.
Seeing that I had had to stop training for the Peninsula
Marathon, I decided that I wouldn't let the frozen
embryos interfere with another marathon. Evan and I
decided to run the Winelands Marathon in the
November, so we would leave the embryos on ice for
the moment.

We so enjoyed our running again and the break from all
the fertility pressure that we decided to train for and

run the Two Oceans Ultra Marathon in Easter 2000. It was good to be putting our energy into something that produced positive results for a change!

I struggled to find the lesson that God was trying to teach us in all of this. I was just grateful that we were being blessed in other areas of our lives. Otherwise I think I would have felt more than a little forgotten.

Chapter Eight

Potentially stay-at-home Mom

In order to get into the position of being a mom who didn't have to work, we needed to get to a point where we could live off Evan's salary alone. This was not going to be possible to do in the neighbourhood that we wanted to live in without some creative strategies. We started looking for a place that had a big enough granny flat for us to comfortably live in, our aim being to rent out the main house. This extra monthly income would enable me to be a stay-at-home mom, my ideal.

Quite miraculously, on a Sunday while I was watching

tennis at home and Evan was on the way back from surfing with a friend, we found our dream home! He had seen an 'On Show' sign outside a house that we had not yet seen in our extensive search. He had a quick look at it and then came rushing home to fetch me to go and see it just before the agents closed up.

It was in Krom Road, Bergvliet and had the potential to be subdivided. We were so blessed by this particular buy as we went to see it on a 'sunshine show house' day. This is when the agents just put boards up and don't advertise in the newspaper. We made an offer for slightly less than the asking price on the Monday and went out for supper. By the time we got home, there was a message on our answering machine saying that our offer had been accepted! The agents called again the next day to tell us that they had received much disapproval from fellow agents in the area who had clients who would have wanted the house at an even higher price.

The house was perfect. It came with a huge garden with lots of trees, a four bed-roomed main house, a swimming pool and a potentially spacious granny flat. The flat was just right for us to make our home in until we could afford to live in the main house. It needed a lot of work but this was fast becoming a passion of mine, so I was only too happy to put my stamp on it!

We moved in October 1999. We spent the first month getting the granny flat ready for habitation – it was just a shell. We did much of the unskilled labour ourselves and even did our own tiling of the kitchen, sometimes cutting tiles late into the night with a noisy angle grinder – the neighbours must have loved us! By the end of the month the flatlet was looking good and suitable for residence. A double carport was later to be added by my father.

Potentially stay-at-home Mom

The house was in a great area as it was near a few good schools and we found tenants easily. We decided to leave the main house as it was so that we could make it beautiful after the tenants had potentially ruined it! The tenant we found told me that she was a landscaper and that if we took a little off the price she would transform the garden. Needless to say, she planted four or five plants and never did anything after that. Fortunately I like mowing lawns and watering, so that became my job.

The granny flat served us well and we ended up converting the attached single garage into a large main bedroom, so we had a small two bed-roomed cottage. Now that we had a secure monthly income from the rental, I was in a position where I could hand in my resignation at Westerford. I was going to start a maths tuition business from home and had a few pupils signed up already from Westerford.

No Kid-ing

I was contacted by Deutsche Schule Kapstadt, a dual medium German school in Cape Town, when they heard that I was leaving Westerford. I didn't want to start teaching at a school again and was excited to be starting up my own maths tuition business. The school really seemed to want me though, so I went in for an interview and negotiated excellent terms. They were happy to pay me a full time salary for a half day job. This meant that I never left after 1pm or coached sport so I could get home and have a quick break before my 3-7pm maths sessions started. It turned out to be a year of hard work with also having to manage the 1500 square meter garden.

With all the renovations we wanted to do, it was a great way to earn a bit of extra cash while we waited for our baby to arrive!

Chapter Nine

The monthly reminder

As planned we ran the Two Oceans Marathon in 2000. It was the first of many marathons, ultra's and triathlons that we would do together in the future. We loved it and running, cycling and swimming had now become a big part of our lives. I am so lucky to have a husband who is comfortable running at the same pace as me. This means that we can do all of our training together and run most of our races side by side.

I wanted to have the embryos put back straight after the race, but Evan and I were invited to Zimbabwe on a ministry trip for two weeks. We had to take Malaria pills which are not to be taken while trying to fall pregnant. By the time the pills were out of my system, it was time for our mid-year holiday. We had saved some money and my brother John who was living in London at the time had contributed some money for us to visit him and also France and Turkey. It was lovely to see him again. Evan and I also had an excellent time together.

During this break from fertility procedures, we were hoping that we would fall pregnant naturally. So many people had told us that if we just relaxed and stopped thinking about it we might fall pregnant. This was always such a ridiculous concept to me. We had physical issues stopping us from conceiving. In our case, it was almost like telling a deaf person to go away on holiday and relax and they would come back with their hearing restored! Sometimes I can't help thinking that people should take a bit more time finding out more about one's actual situation before making unsuitable suggestions.

We were still trusting God for a miracle and our church small group had shown amazing support through prayer and even fasting for us. Every month when my period came, I was disappointed.

I get my period regularly and it lasts for five days and for two or three of these days it is very heavy. Let's do the maths – that means that for 16% to 20% of my so-called reproductive life, I am being vividly reminded that I am not productive in the baby department! Don't even get me started on how much money I have wasted on expensive sanitary products. Maybe someone can tell me why in so many supermarkets in South Africa the sanitary goods are in the same aisle as the nappies and baby products - a bit of a slap in the face!

Chapter Ten

Embryo icicles

When we got back from our holiday, we thought it was high time to give our patient little frozen embryos a warmer home. I had to go on Clomid again to make me extra fertile. Dr Wiswedel said that they would also do an A.I to boost the chances.

Since the last procedure they had managed to increase the chances of conceiving . They used to grow the embryos for two days and then put them into your uterus, where they only implant (attach to the uterus wall) on day five. This gave them three days to hang around before implanting, or as in my previous cases, sneaking out. By now they had the technology and growth cultures to grow them to day five so that when they put them back, they were ready to implant straight away. The chances of conceiving had increased from 33% to between 40 and 50% using this new method. Quite understandably this was encouraging to hear!

When we saw Dr Wiswedel, he explained that they would thaw the embryos, grow them for a further three days and then implant them. I was quite apprehensive as the thought of having these little guys on ice all these months had been quite comforting. We all got into some serious praying again and we were positive and hopeful.

The lab was supposed to call me on the Friday morning to tell me how many of the embryos had survived and at what time they would need to be inserted. They called just before school started and the lab technician explained to me that when they had taken the embryos out of storage the container they were in had exploded. She went on to say that this was very rare, only happens to one in a thousand! She said that some of the embryos had survived the explosion but had stopped growing that morning. I couldn't believe what I was hearing. After all we had already been through, this was just too much!

I called Evan to share the news with him and we were both really down. I had to put on a brave face for the kids at school all day but when I drove home the tears came. I could hardly see where I was going! I got home just before Evan who was at the orthodontist. He had had braces on his teeth for the past two years and was having them taken off that afternoon. We were both feeling really sad when he got home and even a big brace-less smile didn't cheer us up!

Embryo icicles

We still had the chance that perhaps the sperm from the A.I might do the trick, but Dr Wiswedel didn't hold out much hope for this. Well, as usual, I got my period and still no babies. This all happened just before my twenty-ninth birthday.

As a Christian I was struggling with feelings of anger towards God. Why would He withhold the blessing of children from us? What had we done to deserve it? We had a great marriage to bring children into. Many people had said that we would make excellent parents. There I was, a potentially stay-at-home mom, with the two of us ready and waiting to invest in these little lives. I believed that in my relationship with God, as in any normal relationship where someone upset me, I could be angry but I still didn't feel right being angry with my Creator! I remember being comforted greatly by a sermon that a visiting speaker, Dave Holden preached at a conference at our church. His sermon was based on Hebrews Chapter 12 verses 8-11:

[8] If you are not disciplined (and everyone undergoes discipline), then you are illegitimate children and not true sons. [9] Moreover, we have all had human fathers who disciplined us and we respected them for it. How much more should we submit to the Father of our spirits and live! [10] Our fathers disciplined us for a little while as they thought best; but God disciplines us for our good, that we may share in his holiness. [11] No discipline seems pleasant at the time, but painful. Later on, however, it produces a harvest of righteousness and peace for those who have been trained by it.

Dave spoke about testing being a sign of son-ship and went on to say that God gives challenges to people that He thinks will grow and flourish through them. It was a word in season for me and helped me get through many future predicaments without feeling too angry with God! I also developed a good take on an 'eternal

Embryo icicles

perspective' and realised that having children is not what life is all about! After all, our lives here on earth are only a tiny drop in the ocean of eternity.

Chapter Eleven

Miracle evening

Our church small group wanted to see more people being added, so we were trying to come up with an evening that people would be keen to come to. We could all think of a few people we knew who needed miracles in their lives, so we decided to have a 'Miracle Evening'.

I plucked up the courage to invite my mother's hairdresser who had also been trying to have children for a long time. She was very happy to come and even asked if she could bring along a friend who was also struggling for kids. At this stage I had been trying for three years or so, so I also needed a miracle!

We had a great evening with many guests. We prayed for each person who needed a miracle and my guests seemed to have an enjoyable evening. Constance called me about a month later to tell me that both she and her friend were pregnant. I was so happy for them, but couldn't help wondering 'what about me?' I was quite excited for the next few months though as I thought, clearly miracles do happen!

At another stage, a well known evangelist with a healing ministry was invited to come and do a series of meetings at our church. He also had an amazing gift of receiving words of knowledge and being in the meetings was exciting. So many people were healed and came to know Jesus.

No Kid-ing

Simon, our pastor, was hoping that the evangelist would get a word of knowledge for us, but towards the end of his time at our church, he hadn't and Simon thought he would tell him our story so that he could at least pray for us. Simon informed us that he had told him and that he'd said that he would pray for us if there was time. He called Evan and I up to the front of the meeting and unfortunately it came across to most people as if he were bringing a word of knowledge. He is a highly respected man of God, so I know that it was not his intention to give that impression. He simply wanted to pray for us and time was running out. He ended off by saying that when he visited the next year, he hoped to see a baby in our arms.

The church was so excited because of all the other miracles that had taken place. I went to another meeting in a different context and a woman who I didn't even know shouted out across the room, 'So are you pregnant yet?' I was so shocked, I didn't answer. There were many disappointed people when I explained that he knew our situation and was simply praying for us. I wasn't at all disappointed, just extremely grateful that he had made the time for us.

When it comes to women's meetings, I am not a fan. I went to an all girls' school, so I tended to avoid women's only events. I think I had had an overdose of females in my school years! I am sure I would have come around to joining in eventually, but being childless added an even more difficult dimension. When you are in an environment where men are present, there is always someone to talk to when things become too child focused. When you arc in a setting where there are only women, there is just no way to avoid it. When you are meeting new women, introductions usually revolve around finding out how many children one has. That would mean that I'd have to tell some version of my sad story to strangers. I don't mind telling my story, but when you give a summary, there are just too many trite but well meaning comments to deal with.

Friends of mine have asked what the best way is to respond to someone who tells you that they are struggling to have children. That is a difficult one. I can tell you what not to say! Don't tell them to relax and it will just happen and refrain from tales of other people's success stories. Abraham and Sarah references are the worst! Who wants to have kids when they're old enough to be a grandparent? The same level of sensitivity is needed as when you find out that someone has lost a loved one. There is nothing you can say to take the pain away.

Chapter Twelve

The adoption option

We had not yet considered adoption because I had always wanted to see what a little combination of Evan and my genes would be like. Would he have Evan's blue or my brown eyes? Would she be a good musician or a good mathematician? To see a child grow up and develop your characteristics and personality traits was something that we hadn't wanted to give up on just yet.

Because we had been unsuccessful thus far with any of the procedures, we were beginning to wonder if adoption was the route God wanted us to take. One or two of our friends had questioned whether or not it was right for us to have medical intervention if falling pregnant naturally was not happening. Neither Evan nor I had ever had a problem with it. Although there is nothing in the Bible about medical intervention for fertility, there is reference to looking after orphans, so we thought we would start looking into adoption.

A couple that we knew from running had just adopted a baby through a social worker called Wilna Malherbe. We thought we would go and hear what Wilna had to say. We went to see her on our nine year wedding anniversary. The lengthy consultation came at a high price and the estimated cost to adopt a baby was quite honestly beyond us financially. She insisted she didn't want adoption to be something that only the rich could afford, but we had to face that at this price, we were definitely priced out of the market, so to speak.

No Kid-ing

Having initially explored the adoption option because
we'd thought that we'd be following God's heart for
looking after orphans, we now felt that healthy babies
were in such demand that we weren't really solving the
world's orphan problem by adopting. We spent our
anniversary night at the Houw Hoek Inn, so we had lots
of time to discuss what we would do next.

Chapter Thirteen

Third time lucky?

Because the cost of adoption was even more than the price of an ICSI, Evan was really keen for me to try another one. We thought we would go to a different specialist who had been recommended to us by Gustav, a doctor friend of ours from church. He told us that he had done part of his internship with Dr Tregoning, a fertility specialist with an excellent reputation. He worked at the Military Hospital. We got an appointment with him and had a fascinating chat. He was the youngest of the specialists we'd seen. Karen, another doctor from our church, worked closely with him and also spoke highly of him.

The drugs and lab fee were high as usual but fortunately friends of ours had given us a large sum towards this ICSI. They so badly wanted us to have kids at the same time as them! So once again we had to wait for my cycle to start before I could give Dr Tregoning a call and start having injections.

We went into this ICSI with our hopes renewed because two prophetically gifted guys had prayed over us at Summer Camp. On the first night one came to the front to give a word of knowledge. He started by saying that God would give the barren women children – he was reading from scripture. I thought that was quite a strange place to start reading from on a youth camp! On the second night, during the ministry time, we asked him to pray for us. While he was praying, the other one came and prayed too. They were both praying and prophesying things that were pertinent to the procedure. They told us that they strongly believed I would be pregnant in two or three months' time. I felt really pleased as I had needed reassurance that God was behind another procedure and this certainly made it feel like He was.

By now my maths business was doing so well that I'd been able to give up the teaching post at the German school. This really helped free up time for all the coming procedure related appointments. I was used to the injections by now, so they weren't too bad this time around. I only had to have them for seven days as opposed to the usual ten. On day ten of my cycle, I had to go for the scan as usual. I had an appointment with Dr Tregoning at 8am. Evan and I went in and he wasn't there, he was in surgery. They said that they would call me when he was available. This made things a bit tricky, as running my maths business meant that I had five or six pupils lined up back to back every afternoon!

I went in again at lunch time and said that I would wait around. After sitting in reception for about an hour, the receptionist said she would get someone else to do the scan. The lady who was doing the scan was halfway through when Dr Tregoning arrived. He was happy with what he saw and booked me in to have the eggs removed later in the week.

We went to Newlands Surgical Clinic where I had the eggs removed and Evan produced a sperm sample. I had a bit of a laugh as there was a man called Mr Dick who was there for a vasectomy! They removed a record sixteen eggs and I was totally whacked for the rest of the day. The sleeping pills rendered me totally 'out-of-it'!

The next day we were told that they could only work with thirteen of the eggs and that ten had fertilized. I

was going to have them put back five days later. The
night before, I read an amazingly significant Bible verse
in my reading for the day of my One Year Bible. It was
in a fairly tedious section in Exodus, where all the laws
are being given and there it stood:

Exodus Chapter 23 verse 26

> *'There will be no miscarriages or barrenness throughout
> your land, and you will live out the full quota of the days of your
> life.'*

This greatly encouraged me for the days ahead!

On the day that I went in to have the embryos put
back, there was a bit of confusion as to which ward I
was in and they had to call me on my cell phone to
locate me. Thank goodness for modern technology! I
told them I was in D Ward. Marlene, the lab technician
who had recognized our names, told me that the
previous incident where the container holding our

frozen embryos had exploded was only the second time it had happened in her six years at the clinic. She stayed while Dr Tregoning inserted the embryos. It was great to have her there. She was so supportive and really rooting for us!

Now we had to wait one week to find out if I was pregnant. On Valentines Day I went in for my blood test and they said they would have the results by 2 pm. Karen was there and wanted to do a quick urine test for us as she said that one can sometimes tell, even this early, from a urine test. It came back negative and we were quite disheartened, but still hopeful.

Evan and I went out for lunch at the Barnyard Farm Stall to celebrate Valentines Day. When we got home, I called to find out the results after four horrible hours of suspense. Dr Tregoning said that the test was inconclusive and that the number was too high to register negative and not high enough to register positive or something technical along those lines. He said I should come in for another test two days later, but I didn't have to as I got my dreaded period the next day. All those promises - I chose to believe them for the next time around. What a roller coaster of emotion!

Dr Tregoning seemed to imply that the chances were higher if you have procedures done back to back, so we decided to have the frozen embryos put back the following month. He said I didn't have to do injections or take pills. They would do what they call a natural cycle. They tracked my cycle with scans and blood tests and put the frozen ones back five days after ovulation.

When they did the final scan to check on my progress, they weren't happy with the thickness of the lining of my uterus. They thought we should wait for another month before putting them back. We followed their advice, but once again they didn't take.

Third time lucky?

After many well meaning prayers and unfulfilled prophecies over the years of trying to have children, we did become fairly cautious when it came to the prophetic. We had to remind ourselves that prophets are only human and that there were times when they could get it wrong. I am sure that many of these prophets also realized, down the line, that infertility was a particularly sensitive area and one in which they needed to be make sure that they had clearly heard from God. I was also tired of the regular 'Abraham and Sarah' prophecies we had received as I didn't want a baby in my old age, I wanted one 'yesterday'!

Evan and I decided no more procedures until they could actually medically stitch the little guys into my uterus!

Chapter Fourteen

Lodger family

Renting out the main house was good money every month but after a year of teenagers with noisy music, we decided that we could make the same amount in rental if we let out the flatlet and moved into the main house with three lodgers. It was more than conducive to sharing. It had a main bedroom, en-suite bathroom and study in the 'west wing', three bedrooms with a family bathroom in the 'east wing' and a lounge-dining room and kitchen in the centre.

We had a few lodgers staying for short periods but for

the majority of our stay in the house, we had the same three, Bakes, Dave and Ruth. For a good part of the time we had newly married friends, Andy and Louise, staying in the flatlet. Dave had a good friend, Dan, who spent much time at our place and eventually replaced him when he moved out. Although we kept things quite separate, we were like a little family. I was the 'mom' who organised the cleaning roster for the kitchen. Dave, Dan and Bakes all worked at Jubilee with Evan, so they all travelled in to work together every day.

Tuesday nights were 'family nights'. We got a bit of a tradition going, where all of us would gather for hot dogs and a bumper TV watching session with '24', Alias, CSI and Survivor all being watched consecutively.

After five and a half years of trying to have children, we decided that we would look into adoption again but this time through Child Welfare, a government-run service. A good friend of ours, Louise mentioned that she had heard of two babies that had been placed through Child Welfare in the last year. I had previously heard that their waiting lists were closed and so I hadn't even attempted to call. With Louise's news, I thought I would give it a shot.

I phoned them at the end of December and they asked me to call in the second week of January, as they were closing for the holidays. I called on the 8/1/2002 and spoke to one of their social workers, Melanie. She said she would usually say come in for an information session first but based on how keen I sounded, she told me to come and fetch the application forms. She said the speed at which I got the forms filled in would be an indication of how badly we wanted to adopt. I had the forms filled in the same day!

We had to have a medical check-up and blood taken to see that we weren't HIV positive and didn't have any VD's! My father, being a doctor, managed to fast track the results so that we had them the next day. When I called Melanie to ask if I could drop off the forms, she couldn't believe that I had managed to get all the information and especially the medical results so quickly. I think she was impressed. She called and asked us to come for an interview later the next week.

In the interview, she asked us what we knew about the adoption process and we repeated the information that Wilna had told us at our consultation with her. She was impressed with how much we knew and was happy for us to skip the information session. At the end of January we went for our individual sessions. Evan went with Melanie and I went with Avella. They asked loads of questions and took lots of notes.

The next step was the group session early in February. It was a four hour session where we met other couples also wanting to adopt. One lady told an incredible story about how she had gone for an A.I and they had inserted the sperm, but then called her later to tell her that it was the wrong sperm. What a mistake! She didn't fall pregnant and was very relieved.

We also met three couples who had adopted and were sharing their experiences. We had to do role plays and draw pictures about our feelings – all quite new and 'touchy-feely' for us. I felt really proud of poor Evan as this wasn't either of our scene. It was quite funny because we had to draw a picture of how we saw our family and Evan and I both drew pictures of us and our dogs standing outside our house but I had drawn two kids in the picture and Evan hadn't drawn any kids in his!

At the end of the session I went to ask Melanie what our next step would be. Child Welfare was supposed to send letters to two people whom we had chosen as references. We had chosen Nigel Marsh, who is my godfather and had known me since birth and Simon

Pettit, our church leader and close friend. They had to write a letter of reference and send it back. She said that they were waiting for the letters from our references and that we needed to follow up on this. I told her that I had been trying to but that they hadn't received anything from Child Welfare yet. She said she would look into it.

Out of all the people at the session, she called us into her office to speak to us afterwards. I was so excited! She asked us if we minded the birth mother seeing photos of us and if we could get a portfolio together as soon as possible. She said that she would rather give us the letters to pass on to our references than mail them so that we could get it done more quickly, but she couldn't find them!

When I got home there was a message on the answering machine from Procare, another agency that we had approached in the May of the previous year.

No Kid-ing

They had us on their waiting list to be screened.
Previously they had told us that we would probably
only be screened in June or July, but this was a message
to say that they needed to screen us as soon as possible.
I called back and Evan and I made an appointment for
the next day. Procare is based in Wellington, about an
hour and a half away from where we lived, so it was a
long trek.

We met Eloise, the social worker, and once again we
were asked what we knew about the process. We told
her that we felt like adoption experts at that point
because of all we had been through with both Wilna
and Child Welfare! She seemed satisfied that we knew
enough. She said that she didn't want to get our hopes
up but that there was a girl who was eight months
pregnant and hadn't found a suitable couple to adopt
her child yet. She asked us to make a portfolio as soon
as possible. Well obviously our hopes were now up!

From Thursday to Saturday I put all my energy into making two portfolios. I went and bought really nice paper and scanned a whole lot of photos. I went to great trouble and they turned out extremely well. Even I would choose us as parents! Evan wrote a wonderful letter to include, with Perry, one of our earlier lodger's help and my mother also wrote an amazing letter. It took Evan and I three hours to fill out Procare's application form, which was far more detailed than the one from Child Welfare. Some of the questions were quite fun because we had to fill in stuff that we liked about each other.

On Monday we drove through to Wellington to drop off the portfolio and Eloise was very complimentary. We then went to Child Welfare and I dropped the other one off with Melanie. She raved about it and went running off to show people while I was still there! She had in the meantime found the letters to give to our references and passed them on to me to take care of.

Evan and I went to the Mugg and Bean for coffee and then dropped Nigel's letter off at his office. We dropped Simon's one off later at his house and he and Lindsey chatted and prayed with us. Simon wrote an amazing letter and Nigel sent his straight to Child Welfare.

Melanie came for a home visit in the middle of February and she loved our place. She didn't seem at all perturbed that we had three lodgers! I gave her Simon's letter. A week later she called to say that we had made it onto the waiting list and that the next time she called it would more than likely be to tell us that we had a baby.

Chapter Fifteen

Almost a Mom!

Procare had in the meantime called to say that the eight month pregnant mother hadn't chosen us. She had chosen another couple and if she hadn't chosen them, they probably wouldn't have been able to adopt because they were getting older. So we were happy for them.

On Friday, 22/2/2002 at 10:55 am I had just come home from the shops when Melanie called me on my cell phone. I remember her asking me if I was sitting down — I thought she was going to tell me to come and fetch a baby! She told me that we had been chosen to be parents and that the birth mother was due on 04/03/02 – such a cool birth date – especially for a mathematician mom! Only ten day's time! It's difficult to put into words how excited I felt. I called Evan and told him the good news.

All our lodgers were so excited. Evan and I couldn't believe it. It was all too good to be true! Melanie had said that the mother was twenty-six and still studying. Her mother wanted her to keep the baby but she didn't want it to interfere with her studies and she was no longer in a relationship with the father of the baby. We were a little protective of our emotions as we thought she could possibly change her mind.

We went to our friends, Colleen and Johan for supper that night. They had already bought us baby presents! We had accumulated gifts from John, Bakes and Perry. We got the cot that we'd bought in 1998 out of storage and set it up in our room. We couldn't believe that our

long awaited, much prayed for baby was going to be in
there soon!

We had a huge baby shower. Bakes designed a beautiful
invitation for the unisex event. We had about eighty
people at our house and some even had to stand
outside and peer through the window to see us opening
presents. We got loads of amazing gifts! We were so
blessed to feel the love and goodwill from all our family
and friends. It was quite overwhelming and deeply
touching to know that Evan and I weren't the only ones
that were excited for this baby.

Well, the unthinkable happened. Melanie called late on
the Saturday night and asked if Evan was at home. I
told her that he was leading on a youth camp but that I
could get him home immediately. She said that there
was no need and that she would like to come and see us
on Sunday. My heart sank as I knew the next call was
supposed to be the 'come fetch the baby' call. I said to

her that she must please tell me what had happened, as I knew it must be bad news if it required a visit from her. She told me that the baby had been born the day before weighing 1.6kg with a disease called Trisomy 18, commonly known as Edward's disease. She said that babies with this disease rarely live longer than a year. Fortunately the family was going to take care of her. When you are interviewed they ask if you are willing to take a disabled child and we had said that we wanted a healthy baby. It may sound selfish but that is what most first time mothers would hope for.

I couldn't get hold of Evan, so I called my father immediately. He explained that Trisomy 18 is a version of Down's syndrome but that the babies don't usually live longer than six months. I did some serious crying. I was trying to figure out what God was doing through all of this and felt prompted to read the end of Job. I think I was identifying on some level with his sufferings and wanted to see if it ended happily for him. I read Job 42 verses 12 to 14 and was encouraged. It reads:

'So the LORD blessed the latter end of Job more than his beginning: for he had fourteen thousand sheep, and six thousand camels, and a thousand yoke of oxen, and a thousand she asses. He had also seven sons and three daughters. And he called the name of the first, Jemima; and the name of the second, Kezia; and the name of the third, Kerenhappuch. And in all the land were no women found so fair as the daughters of Job: and their father gave them inheritance among their brethren.'

From then on I was also fixed on the name 'Kezia'. The lesson in all these trials was still puzzling!

Chapter Sixteen

Rainbow family

Evan and I were trying to make sense of all of our experiences. We thought that perhaps God was opening our minds to the idea of adopting a baby from another culture and race. I had never been too keen on this before, one of the reasons being that I wanted people looking on from a distance thinking that the baby was ours and not adopted. We had also talked about it with family and there had been mixed reactions

Our group of churches, Newfrontiers, used to hold an annual conference in Bloemfontein which we were attending again at this time. There was a couple that always came to these conferences that had adopted a little black girl and previously I had simply seen it as an act of kindness. When I went to one of the meetings, I saw the little girl, who was by now around eight years old, sitting on her father's lap and it was amazing – I saw no colour, just a dad and his daughter. Through various other themes at the conference, Evan and I felt that God was definitely speaking to us about cross-cultural adoption.

I suppose if you have never struggled to conceive, you don't consider the fact that having children, although instinctive for most, is not guaranteed. So many people speak of having them as though it were a foregone conclusion. I used to!

My reasons for wanting children up until this point had been mostly selfish. I wanted to see what they would look like, to have a baby to love and to love us. The fact that I didn't want everyone to know that I had adopted by just looking at us, made me aware that my motives were partly selfish.

Now I was being challenged. Why did I want children? I began to realise that I should not only be doing it for me but considering the difference we could make in the life of a child born into less fortunate circumstances.

I hadn't got my head around the idea of adopting an HIV positive baby or one with any other health issues. I greatly admire people who do this but think you often find that the people who do are ones who have already raised families of their own and decide to do so with their 'second family'.

Our next challenge was that of winning some family members around to the idea that we would be pursuing cross cultural adoption. I think we succeeded. We now prayed that God would open doors for us.

Chapter Seventeen

Meet the parent

My brother, John had a domestic worker whose daughter was pregnant with her third illegitimate child. Her mother had told her that if she didn't give the child up for adoption she would no longer look after her and her two daughters financially. John told her that Evan and I were looking to adopt and she told her daughter, who then wanted to have a meeting with me.

Before organising a meeting I thought I would give Child Welfare a call to find out what the protocol was for this kind of situation. They said that I should go ahead with the meeting and then refer her to a private social worker, who could manage the process for us from that point.

I met her at the Mugg and Bean restaurant at Cavendish Square. She told me the story of how her mom would cut her off if she had the child and that she couldn't work as she already had two kids to take care of. She gave me a photograph of her recent scan and told me that she had found out that it was a boy. I was a tiny bit disappointed as I had always wanted a girl, probably because I had grown up with three brothers and Evan is one of three boys. I quickly came around to the fact that I would adopt again and when I had thought that I would have four kids naturally, I didn't mind the order, just as long as there was a girl somewhere in the mix.

I told her that the social worker would contact her and that we would be in contact too. The social worker called me once she had seen her and said that all seemed above board. She also told me that it is taboo in African culture to give babies up for adoption, so what they generally do is tell everyone that the baby died in hospital. I was happy about this as it meant that there would be less chance of her changing her mind once she had given her baby up.

There is a horrible law in South Africa and some other countries where the birth mother has the right to change her mind in the first sixty days after the birth of the child. I thought that as she would have told everyone that her baby had died, it would be very difficult to go back on that story. So we wouldn't have to be too worried about losing him once he was born.

The birth mom was due around the time when we had organised a surf trip with two friends. We had only planned to go as far as Port Elizabeth, eight hours drive away, so the social worker assured us that we should not cancel our holiday. She said she would let us know as soon as the birth mom had gone into labour and that we could make our way back home then and be in plenty of time to fetch our baby.

The four of us were having a great time surfing our way up the coast to Port Elizabeth stopping at Stilbaai, Vic Bay, Jeffrey's Bay and Cape St Francis along the way. We made it all the way there and she still hadn't gone into labour. It was now time to head home via Knysna, where we were going to spend a night or two. We arrived at the house we were staying at in time to cook a quick supper and then went to bed.

At about 1am I got a call from the birth mom to say that she was in the hospital. I told her that we would be there in the morning. I woke up our friends and we had to vacuum and clean the place before leaving and I was thinking, 'Hello, can I just go fetch my baby? I have been waiting for him for six years now!' I patiently and excitedly did the necessary cleaning and by 3am we were on our way to fetch our little boy.

The social worker called to tell us that she had collected the baby from the hospital and that we should buy some formula on the way to her house as she had run out. I thought I would get my Paediatrician father to recommend the best formula. After dropping our two surfing friends off and popping in at Pick n Pay to buy some formula, we were on our way to fetch our boy!

We excitedly made our way to the social worker. She warned us that he was a bit squashed as he had been delivered with forceps. She placed him into my arms and I thought, 'This is it.' I still couldn't get my head around the fact that he was actually ours! He didn't look that squashed to me, just a cute little newborn.

We were probably only half awake having just had two or three hours sleep but I guessed that this was going to be the pattern for the next few months anyway, so best get used to it! We named him Zak, as we had by now identified with Abraham and Sarah and thought that a version of Isaac would be appropriate.

Before leaving the social worker's house, we tried to give Zak some milk, but he didn't seem to want to drink yet. I asked the social worker if she thought it would be okay for us to go to Cavendish to buy a carry cot. We still had everything we needed from our massive baby shower. She said it was fine and how we would parent was up to us. So on day one of Zak's little life, he went shopping at Cavendish.

Evan and I were starving, so we stopped for a fast food breakfast and then went to 'Tree House' to buy a fancy denim blue carry cot. We saw people we didn't know very well from church while we were shopping but hid as we didn't want them to be the first people to see our baby. We didn't want news to travel before we had shared the news with family and friends.

Chapter Eighteen

Mom for a day

I called all my family members on the way home with Zak. My brother, John said he would pop around during his lunch time. When we got home, our lodgers had made a 'Welcome Home, Zak' sign. They were all so excited to meet him! Baggy and Chan, our dogs, were quite apprehensive, little Zak would take some getting used to.

He was still a bit restless and I thought perhaps if he didn't want to eat, he might need a nappy change. We apprehensively tackled our first parenting duty. It was a nightmare! By this time John had arrived and we were trying to clean up the mess! Most mothers are lucky enough to have the first nappy changed by a nurse as they are still in hospital. The first one is sticky, like toffee! I think we almost went through a whole packet of wet wipes.

Poor little Zak was cold as this was in the middle of winter! We eventually got him warm and clothed again and then had a bit of a photo session with John. My father and stepmom, Stella were away in Buffalo Bay at the time, so I was quite sad that Dad couldn't be around to offer me all his Paediatric advice!

After John left, Evan and I were left alone to settle in to being parents and all that went with it. Having been away for a few days, and leaving our dogs with the lodgers, it was time for Evan to pick up the much accumulated dog mess in the garden. I wrapped Zak up warmly and was showing him all the plants in the garden, in particular our Strelizia bush which had beautiful, colourful flowers on it. He fell asleep peacefully in my arms and I didn't want to put him down. I went and sat on the couch and just admired my new little boy.

My mother called from work to say that she would come around after work and cook supper for us and while I was on my cell phone to her, our landline rang. Evan answered and I could see he was doing the 'cut throat' mime. I thought that this could only be bad news, so I ended the call to my mom and listened to Evan having what could only be a 'she wants the baby back' conversation. The social worker wanted to speak to me. She told me that the birth mom had changed her mind and wanted to talk to me. I spoke to her and assured her that I was not angry with her and that I understood. I think she may have wanted him back because she breast fed him in the hospital and a bond had been formed. This wasn't supposed to happen. He was supposed to be taken from her immediately. Also, he was her first boy. We told the social worker we would come back immediately.

We drove Zak back without talking in the car. We were both thinking what a crappy day it had been, both literally and figuratively. Evan was amazing once we got to the social worker's house. He said he would like to pray for Zak before giving him back to his birth mother. He prayed an amazing prayer of protection over him. Before she took him, she began saying that as she hadn't planned on keeping him, she didn't have any baby stuff for him. I couldn't believe what I was hearing. She had just taken our baby away and now she wanted our baby stuff too! At this point the social worker quickly escorted her to the back and came through to check that we were okay. We assured her that we were as okay as we could be, given what had just happened and we headed off home.

No Kid-ing

We had just disrupted a wonderful surfing holiday for
nothing, so we decided to call our friends, the Frasers,
in Vic Bay and ask them if we could come back and stay
with them again. We called our two surfing friends and
asked if they wanted to resume the holiday and one of
them did. We went to fetch him immediately and
headed back to Vic Bay. I think it was the best thing we
could have done – a bit of healthy escapism!

The Frasers couldn't believe how well we were handling
the situation. Jenny, a doctor, wanted to prescribe anti-
depressants. To us, it almost felt as if the whole day had
happened to someone else! In a small way, I was
grateful that if a baby was going to be taken back from
us, that at least it had happened on Day One and not
Day Sixty! That would have been cruel.

Chapter Nineteen

Adoption aftermath

After two bad adoption experiences and because it felt like whichever route we chose, we always seemed to be coming up against closed doors, we decided to give the baby quest a break for a while. Obviously we wouldn't use contraception and would continue praying for a miracle. We would just stop the extra measures. We even declined a few babies offered by Child Welfare and Procare.

We felt like we had been through too much and feared that if a mother had to actually take her baby back after sixty days, we just wouldn't cope.

With all the negatives that had happened thus far, it was hard not to believe that that would be our next story, so we decided to avoid adoption all together. We would only consider adopting if the baby was abandoned and they couldn't trace the parents. Then you have the problem though that abandoned babies are sometimes HIV positive and you have to wait a while for the test to prove that they aren't and I still really wanted a newborn.

The adoption agencies kept pressurising us to decide whether they should take us off their lists or not and I eventually said that they should, until we let them know otherwise, which we never have. Closing the door on adoption was hard as it felt like I was closing the door on children altogether. It had taken us such a long walk to get to the point of adopting and then cross cultural adoption, that I was left thinking, 'What now?'

No Kid-ing

We still had all the presents we had received from family and friends at the first baby shower. I started asking various people if they would think it odd if I took stuff back to shops to get the money back. I was concerned that perishables would expire and clothes may be the wrong season by the time a baby eventually arrived. I assured them that I would not expect gifts again along the line, and that I would stock up myself, but all of them emphatically said that they would gladly buy gifts again after all we had been through.

Most of the gifts either came from Pick n' Pay or Woolworths and taking the stuff back was quite a step. Both ladies behind the tills looked at me with a question in their eyes, so I had to explain the story to them. They were extremely sympathetic and refunded me without question – even some of the items that didn't have tags!

Our lodgers had shared so many of the fertility disasters with us; we really had been cemented into a little family.

Adoption aftermath

When the time came for the first of them to leave, the emotions just completely snuck up on us! Time came for Dave's farewell and out of nowhere I felt the tears coming. I made a quick exit to the 'west wing', where I got my emotions in check. I suppose it was the realisation that our little 'unit' was about to be broken up.

The strange thing about the lodger family was that, for us, they were only meant to be a practical way to pay the mortgage. I always wanted to have the house to ourselves, so that we could fill it with our own kids. The lodgers had inadvertently become the family that filled the house!

Chapter Twenty

The dog substitute

Our dogs, Chandler and Baggy both brought us so much joy throughout their lives. Chandler lived until fourteen and Baggy made it to an impressive eleven, which is good for a Great Dane. Because we never had kids, our dogs became very important to us. I'll never forget the kindness of our church, Jubilee. When Baggy died, they sent a big bouquet of flowers in sympathy. Evan took so long to get over her death, our first dog death – it was a difficult time indeed!

I managed to convince Evan that if we weren't going to

The dog substitute

have kids, I needed another dog. I thought a small one
that I could always carry would be good, my own little
'baby'. Having never been a small dog fan, the only
ones that I could think of that were cute were
Dachunds.

I picked up the newspaper and started looking for
puppies. In this particular paper there happened to be
three different litters of pugs being advertised. While I
was growing up, my brother and I used to walk past a
house with a pug that used to bark at us. We always
teased it because it was so ugly. Later on we had visited
a camp site in Buffalo Bay on regular family holidays
and the owners of the campsite had a pug called
Snortjie. I used to pick him up and he grew on me, so
when I was looking in the paper, I thought that perhaps
I was meant to be a pug mom!

Evan warned me that puppies were cute regardless of
the breed, so we should look at the pug parents. He said

that we could go and look at the puppies, but that he'd like us to go away, make a decision and then go back later and fetch one if we still wanted it.

It was love at first sight. I can't believe I wasted so many years not being a pug mother! I was good, I didn't try and convince Evan to buy one there, we came away and discussed it, but by this time Evan too was convinced. He had to lead at a church meeting, but sent me to go and collect our new baby. I took her straight to the meeting in a pink blanket. Someone excitedly came up to me to look in the blanket and I think they got a bit of a shock on seeing that it was a dog!

We called our new baby Feebee and the lodgers loved her! When we took her to my father's house to show her off, he was so sweet. It was like he finally had a grandchild! When I showed him Feebee's baby photos, he asked me if I could get some made so that he could show them off at work.

The dog substitute

This poor pug had no choice but to be the cuddliest puppy on the planet, as broody mommy needed lots of love. She was just so easy to 'baby' as she has never been more than baby size.

Having Feebee truly helped me through so many hard times and I can honestly say that she has made infertility easier!

Chapter Twenty-One

My amazing husband

There were many times when Evan had to lead worship after a failed fertility or adoption attempt. I was always amazed at how well he managed. I would often be too sad and just cry my way through, or I would be too angry at God to worship Him! It has been a journey, but I have learnt to praise God in all circumstances. We had been through our two failed adoption attempts when Evan wrote an amazing song, 'Though the Fig Tree'.

My amazing husband

Here are the lyrics:

Though the fig tree does not blossom,
And there be no fruit on the vine,
When I'm facing trials and troubles,
And I can't make sense of the times

Yet will I, yet will I, yet will I rejoice,
I will rejoice in the Lord, I will rejoice in the Lord,
You are my Hope and my great reward

I have one hope and it's in Jesus,
I have put my trust in God,
You are all I have ever needed,
In the good times and the hard

Let us give thanks to the Lord,
When we are rich and when we're poor
Rejoice in the Lord, rejoice in the Lord
And again I say rejoice.

No Kid-ing

He wrote a short piece on why he had written the song which is based on a scripture from Habakkuk 3 verses 17 & 18. I will include it here:

'This is probably one of my most personal songs. It was born out of Tracy and my difficult trial of dealing with infertility. This led Tracy and I down a very long, hard path of fertility procedures and even two failed attempts at adoption where we lost both babies! Sounds unreal, but it's true.

We have been through years of trying to have children, and now wait to see what God has for us. I have found that it is only through facing trials that scriptures like these become real to you. I can say that I have come to know God more through trial than through easy times. You realise that God is our only source of hope and joy in a world full of uncertainty and difficulty. We just need to learn to find our hope in Him and not what this life can offer us. Our trials are momentary in the light of eternity. Whatever comes our way, we can rejoice because our hope is not in this world, but rests on Jesus.

We are to consider our testing as pure joy because it's producing something in us that only testing can – perseverance. We don't give up.

I remember Tracy being very moved by a sermon by Dave Holden, where he spoke about the Father disciplining the ones He loves. He cares so much for us that he allows us to grow through trials. He doesn't want us to lack character; He is a loving father even when it doesn't seem so. Therefore we can be joyful. For me, joy is an inward knowledge and peace, an assurance that God is for me in all things. Real joy is a Godly confidence!'

Evan has had his fair share of added difficult situations to work through. Initially he had to deal with well meaning, yet insensitive friends asking if he was shooting blanks! He also had to deal with feelings of not being able to give me what I wanted and thinking that I would be better off with someone else. When you enter a marriage as a Christian you become 'one flesh', so there is no *my* problem and *your* problem, only *our* problem. I have also always encouraged Evan that I would far rather be in our wonderful, loving, although childless marriage, than a loveless marriage with children.

Chapter Twenty-Two

Ironman

We decided to make the most of our childless state and threw ourselves whole-heartedly into triathlon. We had been doing shorter distance triathlons previously, but now decided that we would train for an Ironman. This is a race where you swim 3.6 km (2.25 miles), cycle 180 km (112.5 miles) and run 42.2 km (26 miles) consecutively, so obviously it required much time spent training.

Training for any one race would be twelve to sixteen weeks and in the longest week you would be training for a total of twenty-six hours! We ended up doing five

Ironman

Ironman races, two in South Africa, one in Switzerland, one in France and another in Austria.

In both of the South African races I was awarded with podium positions, so all the training paid off. We were having a great time training, racing and making new friends. We were feeling fit and healthy and enjoying having the bodies that go with this kind of commitment. As much as we were enjoying it, my longing for children didn't go away. Unfortunately for me, by this stage Evan was so enjoying our childless life that he was now comfortable with not having kids. So many people have said that this was a coping mechanism, but I know Evan and he was just genuinely over it. Obviously he would still want kids to keep me happy, but he no longer wanted them for himself.

Friends of ours who were also struggling to conceive brought up the donor sperm debate. Evan and I had actually discussed it at one stage and even booked an

appointment with Dr Alperstein to take it further, but
in the end I could tell that Evan was not happy with it.
For me, as opposed to adoption, it was a matter of at
least being able to experience pregnancy and have a
child that would then have one of our genes.

It would also have been so much cheaper than all the
expensive procedures we had already had and unlike
adoption, no one would be able to take my baby away.
The major concern I had was that everyone would
think that it was a miracle baby and I wouldn't want
everyone to know that it was a donor sperm baby. This
would mean that I would have to spend a great deal of
time avoiding these kinds of questions and being the
very open person that I am, it would be hard! And of
course, Evan wasn't keen.

I spent a great deal of time and energy 'working' on him
to try and win him over and debating whether God

would be okay with it or not. I told Evan that of course he would love the baby as his own; after all, he treated our dogs like his own already! He almost came around to the idea, just to make me happy, but I was never going to do it without his total support and I also wasn't too sure about it from a Christian perspective.

Chapter Twenty-Three

Feebee's fertility story

We always knew we wanted Feebee to have puppies, so from early on we were on the lookout for a good male pug for her to mate with. One evening, on one of our run routes, we came across three pugs barking at us around the corner from our house. Their name tags introduced them as Jason, Lisa and Cherry. We made contact with the owners who said that they would be happy to let Jason mate with Feebee, but they first had to get over the fact that Jason was actually a monogamous pug, Lisa being his wife and Cherry their daughter.

When the time came for Feebee and Jason to do their thing, we invited Jason over. The first time he visited, Feebee ran him off his feet, chasing him around the garden and sniffing him all over. She totally exhausted him! The second time he came they had already established a friendship, but Feebee wasn't ready yet. The next time, he brought his whole human family around and we all sat around chatting while they got to know each other better. The owner, Denise, asked where we had got Feebee from. 'Claremont', Evan replied. 'Brevet Road?' Denise asked. 'Yes, that sounds familiar', I said. 'Oh no, you got her from us, Jason is Feebee's father!' Fortunately they hadn't done any mating yet! But it was great to find out that Feebee's mom, dad and sister had moved so close by.

We did have a back-up plan. One of my pupils had pugs, so on Sunday night I called and asked if Yoshi could visit on Monday. He came round and they made friends. He visited again on Tuesday and they mated twice. Now all we had to do was wait and see if Feebs fell pregnant.

I measured her every Tuesday for eight weeks and it was clear from an early stage that she was indeed pregnant. She grew slowly in the beginning, but very fast at the end! Her belly measurements were 49cm, 49cm, 48cm, 49,5cm, 51cm, 52cm, 54cm and then 57cm. In the last two weeks of her pregnancy we could feel the pups moving around and sometimes even see them moving. Feebs carried on life as normal, but she no longer had her energetic and sometimes frightening evening romps with Baggy.

On Thursday, 25 November I could tell that she wasn't herself and was convinced that she was going to have her pups. She was nesting, looking for a good spot to have them. I was really quite nervous as I had a busy teaching day ahead and Evan was working until 11pm.

Paediatric support from my father was also far away in Port Elizabeth where he was on holiday.

As I lay in bed that evening watching TV with Feebee at my side, I could feel her starting to have contractions. I prayed that she would wait until Evan got home. I needed the moral support! Evan arrived at 11pm and the contractions started getting more severe. Just before midnight she gave birth to her first pup. It didn't seem too difficult for her. She bit off the little sac that the pup was in and chewed off the umbilical chord. She gave the pup such a good clean. The second one came within another twenty minutes and she also managed it totally on her own. The third came in another twenty minutes. Here she needed my help. The puppy was out of its sac, but still attached by its chord, so I had to gently tug and break it.

The next one came an hour later and I had to break the sac open, then Feebs got busy cleaning. The final puppy seemed to take forever to come. It arrived just before 4am. I was exhausted, but more so Feebs who needed my help with the sac and the chord! This time I got Evan to cut it properly. All in all she had five beautiful pups, two girls and three boys.

She took very well to the licking and cleaning role, but feeding took a while to come to her, so we had a sleepless morning with lots of whining pups. Eventually Feebee had had enough of the whining and decided it was time for her customary morning cuddle with us. The pups did not like this and made it heard, so I let all five of them cuddle with us in the bed. I think the warmth satisfied them. We helped Feebs feed them in the morning and they all learnt how it worked. They were much quieter, more peaceful pups once they had full tummies! Feebs was looking so skinny now with funny big nipples like udders! She has done so well and we were truly proud of her.

Chapter Twenty-Four

Dark days

The next part of my story is the hardest part for me to put on paper. There are two things that happened to me in my life that revisit me in unwanted flashbacks every now and then and I have to shake them off. Being knocked off my bicycle by a truck is one of them and this next part is the other.

Later on that Friday I took all the puppies to the vet for a routine check up and she did all the necessary checks and declared them healthy. Our domestic worker and gardener always came on a Friday and they were both very excited to see the puppies.

Dark days

By this stage, Feebee was getting better and better at being a mom. She would seldom leave her pups, only to eat and get the occasional cuddle from us. She would spend her time licking and feeding them. They made such cute little noises when they were hungry!

On Saturday morning we had to go for one of our regular training sessions and I was a bit worried to leave Feebee and the puppies alone, but I had been assured by Feebee's breeders that you should leave them to get on with their own thing! We came back from our session to find that three of the puppies were dead and two of them were floppy and weak. We had no idea what to do. We went into crisis mode, trying to find a vet that was open on a Saturday afternoon. I called my mother and she came immediately.

By the time we found a vet, the fourth puppy had died and the fifth one was barely hanging on. Feebee was clearly distressed and had started shaking – we began to worry about her too! We rushed her and her last pup off to the vet. After examining the puppy and hearing about the other deaths, he said that it does happen and is called 'Fading Puppy Syndrome' – same as 'Cot Death' in humans. No explanation for it, but it happens to all of them because they have weak immune systems at this stage and pass whatever they have on by being in close proximity to each other.

The vet said that Feebee was fine, just in shock. He said that the last puppy would not make it. We took it home where I held it in my hands and Evan, Mom and I prayed and prayed for a miracle. After a while I couldn't hold it anymore and handed it over to my mother who held it until it breathed its last. We were beyond sadness. Evan dug a hole in the garden and buried the five lifeless pups in it.

Feebee continued to shake for hours and even on and off into the next day. We didn't go to church on Sunday as we were worried about her and didn't want to leave her. Simon Pettit called after church as he had heard what had happened and Evan just broke as he told him the whole story.

It was a terribly heart breaking experience for us as in some way it was the closest I had become to being a mom – feeling the pups growing in her tummy, delivering the babies, just being a part of it all. I know non-doggy people might think us a bit strange, but when you have been through all that we've been through, your dogs do in a very real way become 'family'.

We debated whether or not to let Feebee try for another litter, but one gets to a stage where you want to protect yourself against more horrible things happening, so we decided to have her spayed.

Chapter Twenty-Five

Left out

One of the worst things about being childless is being left out. Remember how you felt as a child at school when everyone had the latest gadget and you didn't have it yet? I remember I wasn't allowed roller skates and that was hard for me as a ten year old! I understand now that it is decisions like that by my parents that are the reason I never experienced a broken bone until adulthood!

The timing of getting the desired item is also important. The sooner you get it, the better you get at using it! When I got my first yo-yo earlier than my friends did, I could impress all of them with my tricks! So there I was, wanting that latest gadget, in this case kids, so that I could 'fit in' with the rest of my friends who already had them.

Understandably, if you are a family with young kids, it is easier to invite another family with children of a similar age around. It means that the adults can chat while the kids entertain each other. This also carries over to going away on holidays together. It would make things easier to go away with a family with children the same age. Another reason for not inviting childless couples is that some would think that we are less tolerant of children's behaviour – probably true! It does work both ways and I have been guilty of doing the same thing when choosing people to socialise with.

When it came to our entertaining, we would be reluctant to invite certain families around because we didn't know how to entertain their children and our

No Kid-ing

houses have never been child proof. We were also put off inviting people with young kids, when one couple came to visit and one of their children spent most of the time unpacking CD's from our shelves and taking them out of their cases. The wife spent most of the evening trying to settle their younger baby in our bedroom and we were left to entertain the husband and his noisy CD unpacker!

It was later explained to me, that after a long day of miserable kids, if they find something that keeps them happy, you don't care what it is as long as they are occupied. I think this is the reason that people let babies chew and suck on cell phones, remote controls, keys and other valuables. It's fine if they are your valuables, but not my non-gobby ones which I would like to keep that way!

It is true that the longer I have been childless, the more intolerant I have become of bad behaviour in children.

Left out

It takes hard work to raise well behaved kids (and dogs!), so keep up the good work all you responsible parents! Having discussed parenting goals with many friends over the years, it is amazing how many people let their goals slip once children arrive on the scene. Of course this is not true for all!

When I was growing up, my parents took my brother, John and I most places with them. They would give us something to do until bedtime and then with the hosts' permission would find a room for us to sleep in. It seems like everything has become too child-centered these days. I was amazed the other day when we went out to eat at someone's house and the older children were allowed to dish up their food first! Our generation has had it hard as we used to have to wait for the adults, now we mostly have to wait for the kids! When is it our turn?

No Kid-ing

I know it does depend largely on the temperament of the child you have, but I still strongly believe that life as you know it shouldn't stop completely when you have kids. They need to learn to fit in around you! I am not underestimating the challenge involved, but it makes me happy to see well adjusted families. It proves to me that this is not an unachievable goal.

Back in South Africa we only have one set of couple friends without children left, all the others have procreated. They are our easiest friends to be around. All the other friends we have had over the years have had kids. We spend time with many of them, the ones whose kids have grown up a bit are also easy to be around. We find one needs to just 'let go' of those that have babies and young ones, as their focus is naturally child orientated at this stage of their lives. We have found that the friendships often resume later down the line when their kids are older and less labour intensive.

Left out

Amazingly enough, in Dubai, God provided us with wonderful friends who were going through a similar struggle to us and again, it was so easy to spend time with them. Here in Norwich, there are many in my situation and it is so good to no longer feel like I am the only one struggling!

In the past I found it hard to be around people who had children. It would make me feel 'left out'. As I have become more accustomed to being childless, I find it far easier now. Most times when we leave, I think 'That was fun, but thank goodness we can get some peace and quiet!' Do we still have the energy for it? I suppose it is different when they are your own kids. All this leaves me thinking how much easier dogs are than children!

Chapter Twenty-Six

Grandchildren, nephews & nieces

Evan's mother, being the oldest parent, was the first of the parents keen for grandchildren. She has three boys of whom Evan is the youngest, with no grandchildren from the older two. My parents were younger than her and not as concerned because I was the oldest and had married at twenty. My mother had, however, been collecting 'dressing-up' clothes, books and toys for her grandchildren for many years.

When Evan and I were in the thick of our desperation, we didn't give much thought to what our parents were missing out on. I think Evan's mother was the first family member to really feel it. She had moved to a retirement village in Port Elizabeth where most of her friends had grandchildren and were constantly updating her with the latest births and photos to go with it.

During my 'indifferent' stage when I was really trying to convince myself that children were a burden on the planet and just too scary to bring up in today's world, I know I made my mother sad. I'm quite sure she could see through my brave façade. Both of our mothers are 'only children', so I think the appeal of more family around is big for them. I should have been the one to produce the first grandchild as the oldest daughter! And what a Grandad my father would be, being a Paediatrician whose job it is to be good with babies! Seeing him with other people's little ones hurts...

For the moment I am grateful that none of my brothers have children. I know I would find it hard on different levels. Watching friends enjoy the blessing of parenting has often accentuated the sense of loss, but with close family it would be so much more 'in my face'! And then there is also the loss of not witnessing the joy that children born to us would bring to our parents.

The loss of the richness of being three generations sharing significant moments together is hard enough as it is. If I had to be an observer watching my brothers share moments like their children's first smiles, first teeth and first steps with the family, it would be twice as hard. In some ways, it would be nice to have a little nephew or niece to love. I'll just have to cross that bridge when it comes...

Chapter Twenty-Seven

Some dreams do come true

Although I had won the art prize in primary school, I decided not to take art in secondary school, for reasons I cannot fathom. If I had, I would more than likely have studied Architecture or Interior Design, which is where my passion lies. Fortunately, to compensate, I have had the opportunity of designing, renovating and building our own houses over the years. We did extensive renovations on our first two and got to build our current home from scratch. This was a dream come true. How lucky can one frustrated would-be-architect get!

Some dreams do come true

In order to realise this dream, we planned to demolish my father's house which was on a big property, subdivide and build two double storey houses. The process involved moving into his house where we all camped out as various sections were being bashed down. At one stage Dad and Stella, my stepmom, were living in their caravan on the property.

Although it was challenging being onsite, it was fascinating to witness every part of the building process. We built my father's house first and a year and a half later, after having lived in various parts of the house that was being dismantled, we moved into our finished home.

In the design of this house, I didn't factor children into the equation. Obviously you have to think of resale, but we thought it would be crazy to keep designing houses around kids that weren't coming. So we had a 'gym' and 'studio' rather than bedrooms! We built the downstairs as a two bed-roomed, self-contained unit that we could rent out and we had a great open plan space upstairs, which we loved living in. About a month after we had moved in, a friend jokingly asked us when we would be selling. They knew me only too well!

We were enjoying the luxury of our new home, but it did end up costing more than we had expected. This helped us in our decision to seek jobs in Dubai and after six months of living in our house we relocated there with Feebee.

We now own a beautiful property in Cape Town, but currently live in the UK. When it comes to relocating, our home is one of the things that we miss the most. I am still a passionate home-maker, so living in furnished rental accommodation is a bit of a frustration for me. I wish we could be like snails and tortoises and take our own house with us wherever we go!

Some dreams do come true

When most moms would be buying things for their babies, like clothes, toys and books, I would be buying things for my home. When moms were talking about their kids, I was talking about my renovations! I love it when other people are about to renovate or build, and talk about what they are going to do with their houses. This, I can relate to!

Creating great houses seems to be a bit of a common theme with some of us childless people. I suppose it is because we don't have to spend money on children and so we invest it in our properties. Our houses are our 'babies'. When it comes to people showing off photos of kids, I show off pictures of my dogs and houses!

Chapter Twenty-Eight

Fellow infertility sufferers

A couple from church who were friends of ours were going through a similar struggle, but they were not as open about it as we were initially. After a while they shared more with us and it was so nice to have friends we could compare notes with. I was at the stage where I had already had all my procedures and she was just starting with hers. Evan and I had always felt alone in our struggle and everyone we knew kept falling pregnant, so we joked with her that she shouldn't worry about having a child, as everyone we were friends with seemed to conceive with no problem!

I could fully identify with her through every step. Each time she went through an unsuccessful procedure, I would wrestle with my emotions. On one hand I was so sad for them that they had to continue on this hard road that I had walked for so many years, but on the other I was relieved that I hadn't lost a 'fellow sufferer'. Extremely selfish, I know!

The good news for them is that they did eventually have their baby. I think they were far more committed to procedures financially speaking. I am glad for them as she comes from a family where her brothers and sisters have lots of kids. She would have felt very left out!

Recently, one of our best friends got married and we knew that the time would come when he and his wife would try for kids. We had spent so much time together and they were one of our only married friends who still had no children. I had never wanted to ask when they

were going to start trying. In some ways I was dreading
it.

We left for Dubai and there was still no talk of kids for
them. After a few months away, they skyped to share
with us that they had exactly the same problem we had
in terms of their fertility. Now we had very close friends
who could enter our world! In a strange way, it was
comforting – another member of the 'fertility
struggler's club'!

After they had their first procedure, I waited excitedly
to hear the news. She was pregnant! Again, there was
that feeling of joy for them, but then the
disappointment that they couldn't have struggled a little
more, so that they could identify 'a little more'. Yikes!
How could I think these selfish thoughts! Here's a good
analogy to try and justify my feelings. As a chocolate
addict, one would be very unhappy to be in an
environment where everyone around you was being

Fellow infertility sufferers

dished out free chocolate and you couldn't get any, even if you paid a fortune! I am, of course, happy for all my friends that have had kids, but sometimes it feels a bit like not getting any chocolate!

Chapter Twenty-Nine

www.no-kid-ing.com

Since leaving teaching I have enjoyed having more time on my hands. I have enjoyed getting into painting and have even sold a few canvases. Having more time, I came upon the idea of sharing my infertility story through writing a blog. I had kept a journal and several memories from the experience in a box file which I had left in Cape Town in storage. I wanted to get my hands on the material before I started the blog so that I could relay the details as accurately as possible.

We were due to visit home and I was looking forward to getting the material so that I could start with my blog. Our church small group met to have a farewell for us and pray for us to get work visas for the UK. One of the ladies in our group had such a confirming word of knowledge for me. Without knowing anything about my potential blog, she said that she saw me coming back with a folder or file and she thought that God would want me to know that He was behind it.

We enjoyed a long holiday back home with many visa trials, but everything came together in the end. I was excited to begin my blog, but before that, it needed a good name. A friend came up with the name over dinner and then it was all go!

I decided I would publish a small section every day so that people could read it in installments. I wrote it daily and then referred it to friends through Facebook. Some even shared it on their pages too. The response was amazing. What an unexpectedly rewarding experience! Many people seemed touched by my openness. Friends who had known me throughout my struggle felt that they could identify with me on a whole new level.

It has been an affirming and worthwhile task to get my story 'out there'. Through the blog alone, I have 'cyber-met' so many people who are going through similar struggles. A few readers said that they hoped I would turn the story into a book, so here we are!

These days the internet must be so helpful for people who are just learning that they have fertility issues. There is not only the wealth of information available at your fingertips, but also the support groups where you can find others with exactly the same problems as you to connect with.

At the time of my struggle, the internet wasn't around and I wonder if there were even any face-to-face support groups? Funny, back then, not one of my fertility specialists recommended support in any way. It was almost like I was just a part of their 'production line'. I doubt whether I would ever have joined one though. Where there are childless women trying to have babies, there is too much potential for being left out when some of them fall pregnant.

Thank goodness for Facebook! I say this because it is so hard to hear pregnancy announcements and I guess pretty hard for people to deliver their news to me knowing my circumstances. At least with Facebook I don't have to be left out of the loop! That's the good thing, but then I do have to get all the baby photos and regular baby natter! Fortunately over the last few years I have been more stable and accepting of my situation, so I can enjoy the updates, but I can imagine it would have been hard when I was in the thick of my difficult journey!

So many people think that time spent surfing the web or even on Facebook is time wasted. I can honestly say that it has become a great source of encouragement to me personally. I have been able to interact with a new community that I would otherwise never have encountered. I feel all the richer for it.

Chapter Thirty

What now?

The beautiful, solid Beech wood cot that we had bought about six months before we started trying to fall pregnant was the source of much indecision. It was a struggle for me over the years as I kept wondering whether to sell it or not and kept thinking that it would show a huge lack of faith to part with it. I sold it about ten years later, but did so thinking that my child would want a more modern cot when it was eventually born!

Before we started trying to have children, our financial advisor found a very interesting policy that could make people who got pregnant quickly quite a bit of money.

What now?

It was some sort of hospital plan where if you paid a small amount every month, you would get paid out a reasonable lump sum for your hospital stay. You had to have the policy for a year before it would pay out. We decided it was a sound investment.

Problem for us of course, was that it was taking longer and longer to get pregnant! Now we had to debate whether or not to cancel the policy. It was such a tricky decision as again, we felt a bit like we were lacking faith by cancelling. We decided that God doesn't give us brains and logic for nothing and we had to just cancel and realise that it wasn't a successful policy for us. For many of our friends who took the policy and fell pregnant quickly, it was a great investment and they cashed in nicely!

Where had this whole process left me? With our last failed adoption attempt being in 2002, since then there have been times of my still desperately wanting a baby, times of being indifferent about it and only once not wanting one at all. The 'not wanting one at all' occasion happened and for the first time since trying to have children, I was actually relieved to get my period! We were on our way to Dubai and had not factored children into our adventure! It was such an unusual experience for me and as I say, only happened once.

Right now I no longer want a newborn baby, but would love to have children, probably the kind of ages that most of my friend's kids are, between eight and sixteen years old. No, I do not want to adopt at this stage – too many bad experiences on that front. I realise that the only way to have older kids is to have babies that grow into older kids, so yes, on some level, there is still a longing to conceive.

When Evan and I have discussions about children, he reminds me that even if you have kids, they could end up being rebels, causing you nothing but nightmares or even be wonderful, but move to a different country where you never see them. The latter is a very real scenario for South African families where so many parents have lost kids to the foreign nations!

There are so many environmental and educational reasons not to have children. Being a teacher for fourteen years has made me warier of the responsibility that having kids brings. Just observing 11 – 18 years olds in a school environment can be a scary thing. Fortunately, you do get the stars that shine and don't succumb to peer-pressure, so all is not lost. Perhaps this sounds a bit doom and gloom for parents out there, but allow me to enjoy the few positives of being childless!

On an environmental note, we simply do not need any more people on the planet. It is already struggling to support the population it has! Non-renewable resources are not called that for nothing. I know Christians would say that we need more Christian families, but how about going out and making disciples. Again, let me have my little rant!

Clearly, I have to work on buying into the reasons for not having children, because even after considering these things, I still want them. Evan doesn't, but I know he would adapt. One thing that really hurts is seeing him interact with them. Having seen how loving he has been with our dog family and knowing how well he relates to kids, I just know that he would make a brilliant dad.

Having had discussions with other people going through similar struggles and having read other stories, we all have many feelings and experiences in common. There are some differences as to how we deal with our emotions. The good thing is that being in this situation, even if we do not share common emotions all the time, we can always identify with each other.

What now?

It continues to be something that we live with. We are a childless family. Yes, we are still a family – just a small one. I strongly believe that marriage is when you start your family, not when you have your first child. Happily, we are part of God's world-wide family and I know our struggle would have been significantly harder without God as our heavenly father!

It is extremely frustrating living in the UK at this time where it seems like every second push chair has a single, unmarried teenager behind it. At this point I do ask God 'Why?' quite a bit. I trust that He knows the big picture and one day I will look back on my life and understand. But that doesn't really help me with the now. I think back to the story of Job quite often. He had it far worse than me but I am still waiting for *my* happy ending.

The amazing thing is that through this, I still feel loved

by God. I don't feel like he is withholding children from me. I feel more like He is on the sidelines cheering me on for how I am dealing with the hand I have been dealt.

There are so many people that are amazing Christians who have had faith for healing or miracles all their lives and have gone to the grave without their prayers being answered. The wonderful thing for us is that we have a glimpse into what eternity with our God looks like, and there will certainly be no sickness or lack there.

3293242R00097

Printed in Great Britain
by Amazon.co.uk, Ltd.,
Marston Gate.